ANTARCTICA

A Guidebook for Planning and Traveling

Gerardo, Bartolomé
Antarctica!: A guidebook for planning and traveling / Bartolomé Gerardo; fotografías de Paula Ford. - 1ª ed. - Ciudad Autónoma de Buenos Aires: Ediciones Históricas, 2023.
102 p.; 23 x 15 cm. - (Be There / Gerardo Bartolomé; 4)

ISBN 978-987-82942-7-8

1. Antártida. 2. Guías Turísticas. I. Ford, Paula, fot. II. Título.
CDD 919.8904

Table of Contents

Introduction
Antarctica? What do you Expect?

Welcome to our guide

Planning to visit Antarctica? It's a destination that often finds its way onto people's bucket lists after years of dreaming. However, there are a couple of factors to consider. Price can be a concern, and there's also uncertainty about what to expect, making the decision process quite a challenge. It's not uncommon for one person in a couple to be more enthusiastic than the other about the trip.

Some individuals may be convinced about visiting Antarctica, but they still have various doubts. Questions about when to go, how to go, and where to go often arise. We understand these uncertainties and aim to provide guidance in this guidebook. Our goal is to help you evaluate whether to embark on this journey or not, and if you're already convinced, we'll assist you in planning and arranging your trip. Whether it's finding the right time to go or understanding the logistics of hiring a trip, we've got you covered.

Finally, our hope is that by knowing what to expect and having access to numerous tips, you'll be able to have an even more enjoyable trip. Being prepared and informed can enhance your experience and make it truly memorable. We want to equip you with  the knowledge and insights necessary to navigate through your Antarctic adventure smoothly and make the most of every moment.

PAULA AND GERARDO

Chapter 1
How and When

Antarctica is undeniably the most challenging continent to visit, but it is accessible to every tourist. The key factors are financial resources and making the decision to embark on this extraordinary journey. While it requires careful planning and financial investment, anyone with the means and determination can experience the awe-inspiring beauty of Antarctica. In fact in the 2022-2023 season more than 100,000 tourists visited the White Continent!

Antarctica is a vast icy expanse, isolated from civilization, devoid of cities, and protected by the Antarctic Treaty. Unless you receive an invitation from a country with a research base or possess a substantial budget to charter a private expedition, the primary means to reach Antarctica is through a cruise ship. The cruise ship allows visitors to access this remote and pristine continent, providing a unique opportunity to explore its breathtaking landscapes and encounter its unique wildlife.

There are two types of cruises that visit Antarctica. The first type consists of large ships accommodating up to 3,000 tourists, similar to those seen in the Caribbean or Mediterranean seas. These ships do not make landings on Antarctica, and passengers only have a brief opportunity to observe the continent from the ship for a few days. Unfortunately, this means they miss out on the chance to capture stunning pictures of icebergs, witness the diverse wildlife (aside from some distant whales), and truly experience Antarctica. It's safe to say that this type of cruise does not align with the expectations one might have when envisioning a visit to the White Continent.

The second type of cruise is known as Expedition Cruises. These smaller ships accommodate up to 500 passengers, although they usually transport less than 350. They offer trips that last between 10 and 16 days. Unlike the larger cruise ships, Expedition Cruises provide numerous opportunities for landing on Antarctica. You'll have ample chances to capture breathtaking photographs of animals, icebergs, landscapes, and more, while immersing yourself in an incredible experience. It's important to note that this type of cruise is more expensive, with costs ranging from approximately 8,000 to 22,000 dollars/euros per person, depending on various factors, although there might be options as low as 5,000. Throughout the remainder of this guide, we will primarily focus on Expedition Cruises.

As an alternative, we mentioned chartered yachts or small ships. However, it's crucial to recognize that this option is significantly more expensive, starting at a minimum of 50,000 dollars/euros. Additionally, these vessels offer less space and comfort compared to traditional cruises, and they are often subject to more significant sea movements. This alternative is typically reserved for specialized purposes, such as documentary film making or adventurous activities like scuba diving, where individuals are willing to take on more risk. It's essential to remember that when opting for this choice,

you'll be days away from any form of assistance, so careful consideration and preparation are necessary.

The third alternative we mentioned is being invited to visit some of the country bases in Antarctica, and in some cases, this can even be done by plane. However, it's important to note that these invitations are typically reserved for scientists, journalists, or filmmakers who present projects for evaluation. Even if you are fortunate enough to receive an invitation, your access will likely be limited to the base and its immediate surroundings. This experience may not provide the same depth of understanding and connection to Antarctica as an Expedition Cruise would. While visiting a base can be an interesting opportunity, it may not offer the comprehensive Antarctic experience that many seek when traveling to this extraordinary continent.

Who can go to Antarctica?

You might be concerned about your physical fitness for this journey, but there's no need to worry! If you can walk one mile on open grounds, then you can go to Antarctica. The trip won't involve challenging hikes or mountain adventures. Most landings will be on flat or gently sloping terrain, and while you'll be walking on snow, you'll have plenty of time to do so at your own pace. Of course, being in good physical shape can make the experience more comfortable, allowing you to walk faster and feel less tired, but that's the only difference. Age is not a barrier either, as most passengers on board are in their late 50s to late 70s. Cruise companies usually require passengers to present a medical certificate, but it's mainly to ensure you are prepared for being days away from hospital services, not related to the physical requirements of the landings. So, as long as you can walk, you can visit Antarctica!

When to go to Antarctica?

Cruises typically visit Antarctica from November to March/April, but we recommend going between December and February. Why? Firstly, it will be extremely cold earlier in the season, and secondly, for the penguins. If you go in November, you'll be there before the penguins arrive to nest, You might see a few but certainly not what you expect. After February penguins will be starting to leave their nesting places and as March advances you'll see less and less of them, and eventually you'll only be seeing the bodies of those who haven't survived the season. Very sad… Therefore, we suggest going from December to February. During this time, you'll witness an abundance of life in their nesting sites and have plenty of opportunities to take remarkable photographs.

How to choose a cruise?

Choosing a cruise usually starts with considering the price. As mentioned earlier, none of the options are cheap, but you can easily request a quotation from the cruise companies through their websites or your travel agent. In the appendix at the end of this book, you'll find a list of cruise companies for your reference.

Another crucial criterion to consider is the duration of the cruise. Keep in mind that there will be two navigation days to reach Antarctica and another two to return, so you'll need to subtract four days from the total duration to determine how many actual days you'll spend in Antarctica. This will help you accurately assess the length of time you'll have to explore and experience the wonders of the White Continent during your journey.

Some cruises offer the additional option of visiting the Malvinas/Falklands or South Georgia, which can be a fascinating experience. However, it's essential to be aware that this will extend the duration of the cruise with more navigation days, resulting in increased costs. We will delve into this topic further in Chapter 6, where we'll explore various ideas and combinations for your Antarctic journey, helping you make the best decisions for your trip.

While most cruises start from Ushuaia, some depart from Punta Arenas or Puerto Williams. This requires flying from your home to Santiago de Chile instead of Buenos Aires, which could lead to different airplane costs or visa requirements. Before making a decision, it's important to check these details to ensure a smooth trip.

Availability of dates is crucial when considering an Antarctic cruise. The earlier you start thinking about booking, the better chances you'll have of securing your preferred travel dates. It's essential to note that for Antarctica, some travelers book more than one year in advance to ensure they get the dates they desire. So, if you have specific dates in mind, it's wise to plan and book early.

When choosing a cruise, onboard comfort and amenities are essential factors to consider. You can find a wealth of information about the ships' facilities on their websites. Additionally, take into account the size of the ship and the number of passengers it accommodates before making your decision. These aspects play a significant role in ensuring a pleasant and enjoyable journey.

While the landing sites can be an appealing factor, it's important to understand that the locations to be visited will be determined at the last minute due to the ever-changing weather conditions. Therefore, if you choose a cruise based on the promise of visiting a specific location, you may end up being disappointed as the itinerary can be altered for safety reasons. It's crucial to keep in mind that flexibility is key when exploring this unpredictable and mesmerizing continent.

Many individuals consider observing Emperor penguins as very important. While you're certain to encounter Gentoo, Chinstrap, and Adelie penguins, it's essential to note that spotting Emperor penguins is a challenge. Due to their remote rookeries deep inland, they are rarely visible from a ship. Only a handful of cruise vessels provide the option of flying via helicopter to their colonies, contingent on weather conditions and involving a substantial additional expense. If seeing Emperor penguins is a priority for you, it's crucial to choose a cruise company that offers this specialized service.

King and Emperor penguins are quite alike. As another option, we recommend considering King penguins. They reside in South Georgia, the Malvinas/Falkland Islands, and even have a small colony in Tierra del Fuego (200 miles from Ushuaia).

What to pack for Antarctica

Packing for a trip to Antarctica can be quite a challenge, as you'll likely be visiting other places on the same trip, such as Buenos Aires or Santiago. You'll need to prepare for extreme cold in Antarctica, which requires bulky clothing, but also for hot weather, as it will be summer in the southern hemisphere. Packing for such diverse conditions means you'll need a variety of clothing, so try your best to pack as lightly as possible to make your journey more comfortable.

Just in case you were not aware, cruise companies typically provide insulated and waterproof jackets or parkas, as well as waterproof boots. This means you won't have to worry about bringing those items with you, making your packing process a bit easier.

Below is a suggested packing list for your Antarctic adventure:

✓ Thermal base layers: Long-sleeve tops and bottoms for insulation.
✓ Insulated pants and waterproof outer shell pants.
✓ Fleece or down jacket for added warmth.
✓ Moisture-wicking socks and thermal socks.
✓ Gloves or mittens (preferably waterproof) for cold temperatures.
✓ Hat or beanie to protect your head from the cold.
✓ Scarf or neck gaiter to keep your neck and face warm.
✓ Swimwear for any polar plunges or hot tub use onboard.
✓ Casual and comfortable clothing for indoor activities and relaxation.
✓ Sunglasses with UV protection.

✓ Sunscreen with high SPF for protection against the Antarctic sun.

✓ Lip balm with SPF to prevent chapped lips.

✓ Binoculars for wildlife viewing.

✓ Camera or smartphone with extra batteries and memory cards and a waterproof and shockproof phone case or pouch.

✓ Power adapters and chargers for your electronic devices. Find out what are the connectors in the ship because you might need to take adaptors.

✓ Waterproof dry bags to protect your belongings during wet landings.

✓ Small backpack for carrying essentials during excursions.

✓ Travel-size toiletries and personal hygiene products.

✓ Prescription medications and any necessary medical supplies like Dramamine (remember that there are no drugstores around!)

Remember to check with your cruise operator for any specific recommendations or requirements they may have regarding clothing and equipment.

Conclusion

The best and most affordable way to truly visit and experience Antarctica is through an Expedition Cruise. There are no specific physical requirements, but being in good health is essential as you'll be far from medical facilities. Your trip will take place during the Antarctic summer (winter in the Northern hemisphere) and will last between 9 and 18 days. The estimated cost per person can be between 10,000 and 20,000 dollars/euros, but there might be "last-minute" opportunities available.

Plan and prepare your trip well in advance.

Chapter 2

What's an Antarctic Expedition Cruise Like

Time is money, they say, particularly considering that a single day on an Antarctic cruise carries a price tag of approximately 800 dollars/euros! The White Continent is located several hundreds of miles away from any inhabited land, necessitating a minimal duration for the navigation to and from Antarctica. By examining the map and considering that your visit will focus on the Antarctic Peninsula, it becomes clear why expeditions commence from Tierra del Fuego. The strategic proximity of Tierra del Fuego to the Antarctic Peninsula facilitates efficient and expedient access to this remarkable region.

Ushuaia, situated in Argentina, serves as the preferred gateway to Antarctica for 90% of cruise operators. Its strategic location not only minimizes navigation time but also boasts a secure harbor and a dependable airport that accommodates large aircraft carrying hundreds of tourists from across the globe. Moreover, Ushuaia is equipped to meet the diverse needs of these cruises, providing essential resources such as fuel, provisions, and other necessities.

A select few ships opt for Punta Arenas or Puerto Williams in Chile as their departure points. However, the majority of vessels favor the Argentine city for several reasons. Firstly, choosing Punta Arenas would entail an additional two days of navigation, which is a significant factor considering the value of time in this context. Secondly, Puerto Williams' airport is not equipped to handle large airplanes, resulting in complications during the boarding and offboarding processes for tourists. These factors contribute to the prevailing preference for Ushuaia as the optimal starting point for Antarctic expeditions.

Every day, approximately five expedition cruises conclude their Antarctic trips in Ushuaia, while an equal number of new cruises embark on their

journeys, welcoming an average of two to three hundred passengers each. Consequently, nearly two thousand individuals arrive and depart from Ushuaia daily, forming a bustling stream of visitors to the magnificent expanse of the Big White. Ushuaia, a captivating city abundant with attractions and activities, warrants further exploration as we will see in Chapter 6.

When planning your Antarctic journey, it is likely that you will depart from Ushuaia. As a result, you will be flying from your hometown to Buenos Aires (we highly recommend spending a couple of days there to explore). On the morning of your Antarctic adventure, you will board a three-hour flight to Ushuaia, where representatives from your chosen cruising company will warmly welcome you and handle your luggage. They will then transport you directly to the ship.

If you opt to depart from Punta Arenas or Puerto Williams, the main difference is that you will arrive in South America via Santiago de Chile instead of Buenos Aires. Regardless of your departure point, we suggest considering a minimum of two days in either Santiago or Buenos Aires. Both cities possess captivating beauty and offer a wealth of fascinating attractions that deserve to be experienced firsthand.

Antarctica 21 is a unique cruise company that offers a different alternative for tourists: You fly from Punta Arenas directly to the White Continent (and back), eliminating the need for the two-day navigation across the Drake Passage. This allows you to maximize your time exploring the wonders of Antarctica.

South Shetland Islands will be your first sight of Antarctica

The adventure starts

On the bus, you'll have the opportunity to meet your fellow travelers and engage in exciting conversations about Antarctica. With the knowledge gained from reading this guide, you'll likely feel less anxious than others, as you'll have a better understanding of what to expect from the trip.

Once on board, the crew will provide essential information about life on-board, but most importantly, you'll be assigned a cabin. The size and comfort of the cabins can vary significantly between ships, but most cruises offer spacious and comfortable accommodations. Your cabin will likely feature a desk, which is particularly useful if you bring along your computer, a television for viewing videos and briefings, and, of course, comfortable beds and a large window.

As for onboard amenities, they differ from ship to ship, but many offer a range of facilities such as a gym, jacuzzi, bar, restaurant, lounges for relaxation and interaction with other passengers or the expedition team, observation decks, lecture rooms, and, importantly, Wi-Fi access to keep in touch with the outside world and your friends and family.

During the first two days, you'll navigate the notorious Drake Passage, which may result in some ship movement and possible seasickness. However, rest assured that the conditions will change once you reach Antarctica. If you don't feel well, you can choose to stay in your cabin, although you may miss a few lectures, it won't significantly impact your Antarctic experience.

Towards the end of the second day, you might catch sight of distant icebergs and pristine ice-covered islands, but the true essence of your Antarctic adventure begins on the third day. It is at this point that your genuine Antarctic experience truly unfolds.

During the initial two days, passengers will be organized into groups to facilitate the planned landings. You'll also be provided with boots for your Antarctic explorations. As part of the conservation efforts, you'll have to vacuum your clothing to ensure you don't inadvertently carry small seeds or foreign materials to this pristine continent. These measures are taken to protect the unique and delicate ecosystem of Antarctica and maintain its natural beauty for future generations to enjoy.

A day in Antarctica

Finally, the ship will arrive to Antarctica...

During your Antarctic expedition, you can expect to have one or two activities every day, which may include landings or zodiac cruising. The ship's size plays a significant role in determining the number and types of activities available.

Landings in Antarctica are subject to strict regulations governed by International Association of Antartica Tour Operators (IAATO) protocols. One such regulation pertains to the maximum number of passengers allowed on land simultaneously, typically set at 100 individuals, although certain locations may impose a lower limit of 60. This becomes a logistical consideration for larger ships that can accommodate 300 to 400 passengers, as it necessitates the implementation of "shifts" to facilitate landings. Each shift typically lasts around 90 minutes, resulting in a total duration of 4 to 5 hours for all passengers to complete their landing, leaving limited time and energy for additional activities.

Conversely, smaller ships with a capacity of 100 to 200 passengers require a shorter duration of 2 to 3 hours for landings, thus allowing for more time and opportunities to engage in various activities throughout the day.

Consequently, smaller ships offer a greater range of experiences and possibilities during the Antarctic journey.

The great thing about the Antarctic summer is that the days are incredibly long. This means that if the locations are close to each other, even larger ships can sometimes offer two activities in a single day. Usually, you can expect a morning landing followed by a zodiac cruise in the afternoon. This gives you ample opportunities to explore and experience the wonders of your trip, making the most of every moment.

Landings

As we mentioned before, the Drake Passage can be a bit tricky due to the possibility of the ship moving. However, once you're navigating in Antarctica, the ship will usually sail between the Antarctic Peninsula to the east and the surrounding islands to the west. As a result, the waters are generally calm. This is particularly important when it comes to landings, as you'll be using zodiac boats to reach the shores of Antarctica. Quiet waters make the landings much smoother and safer, allowing you to step on land with ease and excitement.

Before each landing, there will be a briefing where you'll receive detailed information about the landing site, what you can expect to see, and other important instructions. As part of your designated group, you will be called to the meeting area on the ship, where you'll board a zodiac for the excursion. The experienced expedition team members will be present to assist you throughout the process. It's crucial to follow the safety guidelines carefully. Boarding the zodiac is usually straightforward, but the actual landing on the shore can be a bit trickier due to the changing conditions. Rest assured that the team will guide and ensure a safe and memorable experience.

Typically, the navigation to the landing site is relatively short, usually around 15 minutes. While choppy seas are rare, you may encounter cold, strong winds, and some splashing water. It's essential to dress appropriately for these conditions, ensuring you stay warm and protected during the zodiac ride. Wearing suitable layers, waterproof clothing, and a good quality windproof jacket will help you stay comfortable and enjoy the experience without any discomfort from the weather.

As mentioned earlier, landing can be a bit challenging as you may need to step out of a moving zodiac onto rocks or a beach. However, you need not worry, as the members of the Expedition team will be there to assist you. Before disembarking from the zodiac, make sure to carefully listen to their instructions and follow their guidance. They will provide essential safety guidelines to ensure a smooth and enjoyable landing for everyone. Your safety is their top priority, so trust their expertise and guidance.

Once you step onto land, you'll have the opportunity to explore either a designated trail or an open area. The Antarctic landscape offers a diverse range of attractions to see and activities to enjoy. At the end of this

24

guidebook, you'll find an index listing various landing sites and the unique features of each location.

During your landings, you can expect to encounter captivating sights such as penguin rookeries, breathtaking viewpoints, old historic stations, mesmerizing ice formations, and majestic glaciers. Each site holds its own wonders waiting to be discovered.

While exploring, it's essential to abide by the IAATO protocols, which prioritize the preservation of the delicate Antarctic environment. You'll be kindly requested not to sit on ice or snow, refrain from picking up rocks or any natural elements, and maintain a safe distance of at least 15 meters from the wildlife you may encounter. These guidelines are crucial in ensuring the protection of this pristine ecosystem for future generations to enjoy.

After spending around 60 to 90 minutes exploring the landing site, it will be time to head back to the designated point to board the zodiacs and return to the ship. The procedure for boarding the zodiacs is similar to when you first disembarked, with the assistance of the expedition team.

Once you're back on the ship, there is an essential rinsing process for your boots. This is a crucial step to prevent any potential transfer of dust, fungi, or bacteria from one landing site to another. By taking this precaution, we

Camping in Antarctica

ensure that we preserve the pristine environment and protect the unique ecosystems of each landing location.

Depending on the capacity of the ship and the maximum number of visitors allowed on a landing site at once, there may be multiple shifts for the landings. If you find yourself waiting on board during one of these shifts, there's no need to fret. The expedition team has got you covered with organized activities to keep you engaged and entertained.

They usually host informative lectures or workshops that cover a range of topics related to the Antarctic region, wildlife, geology, history, and more. These sessions are not only educational but also highly enjoyable, providing you with fascinating insights into the wonders of the region.

So, even during the moments you're not on land, you'll still be fully immersed in the experience and learning. Plus, these activities offer an excellent opportunity to meet fellow passengers, share stories, and make new friends who share your enthusiasm for the White Continent.

Zodiac Cruising

This is another exciting activity you'll get to experience. While not physically demanding, it does require some endurance, mainly due to the cold weather and the chance of getting wet. Despite the challenges, it is a highly rewarding experience that you wouldn't want to miss.

During the Zodiac Cruise, be sure to have your photography gear ready as you'll sail through breathtaking scenery surrounded by massive icebergs. Keep a keen eye out for seals, particularly on the flat sea-ice formations, as they often bask in the cold Antarctic waters.

The duration of this activity is typically around 45 minutes, and just like landings, it's organized in shifts based on the groups. The expert guides and crew members will ensure your safety and provide valuable insights about the incredible sights you'll encounter during the cruise.

Other activities

Many cruises offer additional activities that may come with an extra cost or require prior sign-up (or even a lottery!). These options provide unique

experiences and opportunities to explore Antarctica in different ways. Here are some of the activities you might find:

• Kayaking – This activity usually takes place while others are on land, so it may coincide with a landing site. However, kayaking is highly weather-dependent and may not always be possible.

• Snowshoeing – Also performed while the main group lands but in this case, you will also land except that not on the exact same spot. This activity can be physically demanding, and participants should be able to handle a 5-mile hike (8 km).

• Camping - Many people come to Antarctica with this dream to be fulfilled, so there will be many more people on the list than the actual possibilities of camping. What is it about? You'll land around 9 pm and, with the help of the expedition team, you'll pitch your own tent. Nights are very cold, but you'll have everything to enjoy a great time. Remember that in summer there are almost no real night hours. Very early in the morning the group will wake up to undo their tents and come back to the ship in time for a hot breakfast. A truly memorable experience!

- Photography groups – Either when landing or when zodiac-cruising, there will be a group that will be leaded by the on-board photographer and, usually, this group will have a separate previous briefing and a later workshop to select and edit the photos.
- Polar Plunge - In select landing sites with ideal conditions, the expedition team may organize a polar plunge challenge. Brave participants can take a brief dip in the frigid Antarctic waters, earning a special diploma for their courage.
- Science group – Some passengers can share the Zodiac or landing group with some of the scientists that usually are part of the cruise. This activity is perfect for wildlife enthusiasts and those interested in science and environmentalism.
- Submergible – Certain cruises offer the incredible opportunity to explore underwater life using a small submarine. Witness the diverse marine world beneath the Antarctic waters, providing an extraordinary experience.

Keep in mind that availability for these activities might be limited, and some may depend on favorable weather conditions. Before your trip, check with your cruise company about the specific activities offered during your cruise.

Other onboard activities, thoughtfully arranged by the Expedition Team, include:

- Bird Watching: Join the ornithologist on deck for birdwatching sessions, where you can spot various bird species soaring through the skies.
- Whale Watching: While not officially scheduled, the Expedition Team will announce any whale sightings, giving you a chance to witness these majestic creatures in their natural habitat.
- Informative Lectures: Enjoy captivating lectures conducted by knowledgeable members of the Expedition Team or guest lecturers. Learn fascinating facts about Antarctica, its history or its unique ecosystem.
- Engaging Workshops: Participate in workshops covering various themes, some related to Antarctica, while others might explore different topics of interest.

These activities provide enriching experiences and opportunities to learn more about the mesmerizing world of Antarctica and its incredible wildlife. Be sure to make the most of these onboard offerings during your expedition cruise!

Chapter 3

What is
Antarctica About

You've likely been contemplating (and perhaps daydreaming) about Antarctica for quite some time. You may have wondered if the experience truly justifies the expense. Maybe you're already convinced, or close to it, about embarking on this adventure. But do you have a clear understanding of what awaits you there? In this guide, we will do our utmost to provide you with a comprehensive explanation.

The first description would be that Antarctica is like another planet. It's unlike anything you know or any place you've visited before.

Even during the summer, Antarctica remains mostly covered by ice. The landscape is predominantly white, except for the sea and the rocks of some very steep mountains. This is why it's often referred to as the White Continent, Big White, or the White Desert.

Antarctica is devoid of trees, bushes, or grass. In rare spots free of ice or snow, you might come across some moss or lichens, which represent the limited plant life on the continent. However, there is more to the story, as we will explore in the upcoming chapters.

The sea around Antarctica is unlike any typical sea due to the presence of countless floating icebergs. These icebergs may appear large, but astonishingly, they only reveal about 10% of their actual volume. They are ten times bigger than they seem! Their captivating shapes and intricate designs are truly mesmerizing as they slowly melt. You'll find yourself wanting to spend hours gazing out of a window, observing this breathtaking landscape unfold before your eyes, as if it was a fascinating documentary.

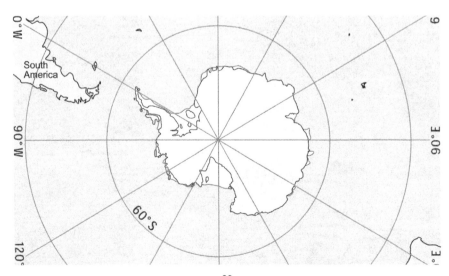

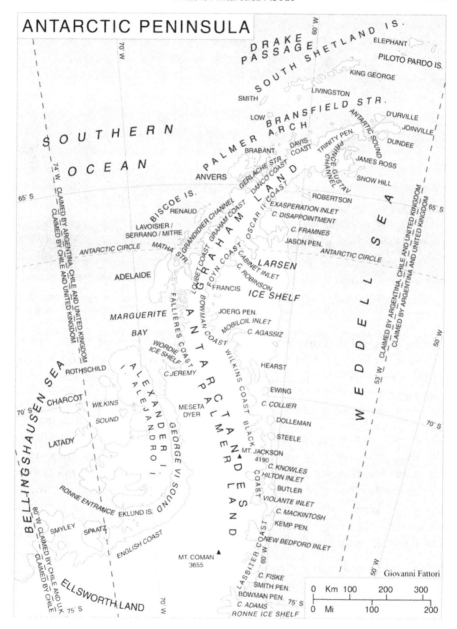

ANTARCTIC PENINSULA

Despite the seemingly lifeless beauty, Antarctica is far from dead. As you explore, you'll discover a vibrant world of wildlife, and you'll be eager to identify the various animals and understand their crucial roles in Antarctica's life cycle. In the following chapters we'll delve deeper into the fascinating and thriving ecosystem of this remarkable continent.

During your ship's journey, you'll have the chance to spot whales, seals, penguins, and various bird species. Upon landing, you'll be greeted by lively penguin colonies and the watchful skuas, creating an unforgettable wildlife spectacle.

An Antarctic trip offers much more than just observing from a distance. It's about fully immersing yourself in the experience. When you step outside the ship, you'll embrace the cold weather as a part of the journey, not a hardship. The freezing breeze and ocean spray on the zodiac will remind you of the harshness of this region. On land, walking will keep you warm, but if you pause, you'll feel the cold creeping in, making it an authentic experience. Camping will offer an even deeper connection to the environment and the true essence of Antarctica.

Indeed, exploration and discovery are at the heart of the Antarctic experience. As you scan the vast sea for whales, penguins, or mesmerizing icebergs, the sense of exploration will thrill you. And when you find what you sought, the feeling of discovery will be incredibly rewarding. Antarctica offers an abundance of both, making your journey unforgettable.

In this chapter, we'll explore the fundamentals of the Antarctic ecosystem, helping you understand and appreciate the incredible sights before you. By gaining insight into this unique environment, you'll develop a deeper connection to the wonders of this region.

The Antarctic Continent

As you can observe on the map, we can divide the White Continent into two distinct parts. The circular region, nearly centered around the South Pole and entirely within the Antarctic circle, is what we refer to as the Antarctic Mainland. On the other hand, the peninsula that stretches towards South America is known as the Antarctic Peninsula.

The Antarctic Peninsula and the tip of South America

35

The Antarctic Mainland is primarily a plateau that accumulates snow year after year. Due to the intensely low temperatures, the snow does not evaporate, causing it to accumulate and gradually transform into solid ice. Although the continent is not entirely flat, it is covered by a thick layer of ice, approximately one mile deep, making it look flat like a plateau.

The immense pressure forces the ice to move, flowing towards the edges of the continent, creating enormous glaciers or ice shelves that can extend for hundreds of miles. Examples of these are the Ross and Weddell ice shelves.

A simple comparison for the Antarctic Mainland is to visualize it as an overflowing bathtub. It's filled with so much ice, and receives more from the atmosphere, that it overflows and breaks away from the ice barriers, creating massive floating icebergs that drift for decades before finally melting away.

The vast amount of ice on the Antarctic Mainland creates a significantly colder climate compared to the Northern Pole. Its cold influence extends beyond the Antarctic circle, reaching the Antarctic Peninsula and even further north into Patagonia.

The geography of the Antarctic Peninsula differs significantly from the mainland. It is characterized by a mountainous range that extends far beyond the Antarctic Circle. The peninsula boasts thousands of glaciers that descend from the mountains, producing massive icebergs as these ice rivers reach the ocean. While many glaciers worldwide are shrinking due to the effects

of global warming, the glaciers on the Antarctic Peninsula appear to be far more resilient in the face of these changes.

During winter, the upper portion of the sea surrounding Antarctica freezes, resulting in a doubling of its surface area. When you visit the White Continent, you will learn to distinguish between icebergs originating from glaciers and sea ice. Glacier-derived icebergs exhibit a distinct cobalt blue hue and resemble mountain-like formations, whereas sea ice appears whiter and flatter. This distinction plays a significant role in the fauna you will encounter during your journey.

Antarctic Life

When you think of Antarctica as a continent, you'll be surprised by its low diversity of life. Any county in the US contains many more animal species than this entire continent. How can that be?

In addition, the Antarctic Mainland holds almost no animals at all. Explorers such as Amundsen, Scott, or Shackleton reported seeing no animals for weeks while crossing the Antarctic plateau. The reason is that there are no plants, and therefore, nothing for animals to eat. Life in Antarctica is mainly centered around the sea. Why? Because the sea here is teeming with life.

Air temperatures in Antarctica can drop as low as -80 degrees Celsius / -112 °F), but sea water does not go below -2 degrees Celsius (28 °F). This means that the water is relatively warm compared to the extreme cold of life on land.

By the end of winter, Antarctica is surrounded by millions of square miles of sea ice. Under this ice, there are species of algae that can survive and photosynthesize sunlight. It's incredible to think that there are millions of square miles covered with algae! This abundance of algae creates a vast food source that is utilized by a small shrimp-like crustacean called krill. In the Antarctic waters, there are literally billions of krill, and they play a crucial role in the ecosystem. Many larger animal species, such as whales, seals, sea birds, penguins, and fish, depend on krill as their primary food source. And in turn, there are other species that feed on them, making Antarctica a delicate and interconnected ecosystem absolutely krill dependent.

During your visit to the Antarctic Peninsula, you'll have the opportunity to see many of these fascinating species. To make it easier for you, we have compiled a list of these animals in our appendix. Additionally, we are currently working on an Observation Guide of Antarctic Fauna, which will be available soon to enhance your wildlife viewing experience.

Chapter 4

Past and Present
of the White Continent

Geologic history

Antarctica's geologic history is truly fascinating, stretching back millions of years. Just like other continents, it was once part of the supercontinent Pangea and later the Gondwana. Over time, it went through numerous tectonic events. During the Paleozoic era, it was located closer to the equator, supporting a wide array of life. As Gondwana broke apart, Antarctica started moving southward and eventually became encased in ice approximately 34 million years ago. Finally, around 15 million years ago, it completely separated from South America. This remarkable journey has shaped the continent into the unique and remote icy landscape we know today.

Over time Antarctica's ice sheet has waxed and waned throughout the Cenozoic era, preserving evidence of ancient climates and fossils. The continent's geology boasts impressive features such as the Transantarctic Mountains and the West Antarctic Rift System. As a crucial location for studying Earth's history, climate change, and geologic processes, Antarctica continues to provide valuable insights into the complexities of our planet's past and present. Its icy landscape holds a treasure trove of information that scientists eagerly explore to deepen our understanding of the world we inhabit.

Humans discover Antarctica

Back in the 16th century, old maps, including Ortelius' from 1570, depicted land in the Antarctic region. However, European nations were not yet aware of the actual existence of the continent. The concept of balance, influenced by classical Greek philosophers, led map makers to speculate that if there was more known land in the Northern hemisphere compared to the Southern hemisphere, there must be a substantial undiscovered continent to restore equilibrium. They named this hypothetical landmass "Antarctica," positioned opposite the Arctic at the North Pole. It wasn't until much later that the true nature of Antarctica was revealed through exploration and scientific study.

In 1768, Captain Cook became the first explorer to encounter evidence of land in the far south. During his voyage, he observed icebergs with rocks, and dust on the ice, leading him to deduce that glaciers were present,

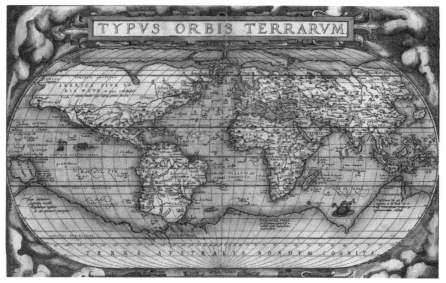

Ortelius' World Map from 1570

indicating the existence of land in the southern region. However, at that time, the idea of an ice-covered continent did not seem appealing to the rich nations seeking new territories to inhabit. Consequently, there were no immediate expeditions sent in that direction as they preferred to focus on more promising prospects elsewhere.

During the early 19th century, the southern hemisphere fur seals were found to be highly valuable for their fur, leading to intense hunting in regions like Patagonia and the southern Atlantic islands. As a result, the seal population was nearly decimated. However, as the sealers ventured farther south, they stumbled upon Antarctic islands where the beaches were teeming with thousands of fur seals. Exploiting this new resource, they continued hunting on these crowded shores until the seals were almost entirely wiped out.

It was during this period of exploration and sealing that some adventurous explorers circumnavigated Antarctica, gradually confirming its status as a continent. The discovery of these vast seal colonies and the quest for economic gains played a significant role in uncovering the true nature of Antarctica and its immense expanse.

As the fur seals were hunted to near extinction and their economic value diminished, the motivation for further exploration of the extreme south also dwindled. Without the prospect of valuable resources or profitable ventures, expeditions to Antarctica became less appealing to nations and individuals. The harsh and inhospitable conditions of the continent, combined with the lack of economic incentives, discouraged further large-scale exploration for several decades.

Another reason that discouraged explorers from venturing into the extreme south was the perilous navigation among icebergs using sailing ships. These ships heavily relied on the wind to determine their direction, making it risky to avoid collisions with icebergs. However, in the late 19th century, a technological breakthrough occurred with the introduction of hybrid ships. These innovative vessels combined traditional wind sails with powerful steam engines, revitalizing polar explorations and providing explorers with newfound opportunities to navigate relatively safely through icy waters.

The Heroic Age of Antarctic Exploration

The White Continent, often called the "last frontier," captivated the attention of newly established geographic societies worldwide. As a result, numerous expeditions were launched with a scientific purpose to explore Antarctica. Some notable examples include the Belgica and the Nordenskjold expeditions. Although these ventures found themselves trapped in ice and had to endure harsh winters, they managed to gather crucial data and insights about life and weather in the polar regions. Their efforts proved invaluable in advancing the understanding of this remote land.

Scott's tragic expedition

Historic sites can be seen along the coast

Over time, the focus of Antarctic expeditions shifted from purely scientific endeavors to a competitive quest known as the Polar Race. When Ernest Shackleton's expedition in 1909 fell short by only 100 miles from reaching the South Pole, the possibility of claiming the coveted prize became more tantalizing than ever before. The pursuit of being the first to conquer the South Pole ignited a new era of exploration and adventure in Antarctica.

Amundsen's expedition reaches de South Pole

Tragic Race to the Pole

In 1910-1911, two expeditions were organized with the ambitious goal of reaching the South Pole. One was led by Robert Scott from the UK, and the other by Roald Amundsen from Norway. Remarkably, both expeditions successfully reached the exact South Pole. However, Amundsen's team achieved their triumph nearly a month ahead of Scott's. Tragically, Scott's return journey proved fatal, as he and his companions succumbed to the harsh Antarctic winter. Their fate remained unknown until a year later when their remains were discovered.

Shackleton's Endurance Expedition (1914-1917)

Shortly after Scott's diary was published, Shackleton proposed his plan to cross Antarctica by passing over the Pole. His ship, the Endurance, became trapped in the frozen sea-ice and was eventually destroyed by the pressure. The men survived by camping on drifting ice and later sailed on whale boats to Elephant Island. Shackleton and a small group sailed another 800 nautical miles to South Georgia to seek help. Everyone from the Endurance expedition was rescued.

Shackleton's *Endurance* caught in the ice

Shackleton passed away a few years later (1922) while organizing another expedition in South Georgia, and he was laid to rest there.

Sovereignty Claims

During the Heroic Age, the discovery of fossils in Antarctica provided evidence of its ancient forests and animal life. This finding sparked interest in the continent's potential for carbon and petroleum reserves, a valuable resource for energy-hungry nations undergoing rapid industrialization.

In 1904, Argentina established a permanent station on the South Orkney Islands, followed by other countries like Chile, the USA, and the UK, leading

Boats from the old days

The Historic British station of HorseShoe Island

The old station of Horseshoe island can be visited

to the presence of more than fifty research stations from twelve nations, mostly located on the Antarctic peninsula.

Tensions arose as Argentina, Chile, and the UK claimed sovereignty over the peninsula and other countries staked overlapping claims in different areas. Despite these assertions, many nations chose to disregard these territorial claims. After World War II, the stage was set for a potential conflict over Antarctica.

Antarctic Treaty

In 1949, Argentina, Chile, and Great Britain, all having overlapping claims on the Antarctic Peninsula, signed a declaration agreeing not to deploy warships to the region. Despite this commitment, there were still several conflicts over the occupation of the area.

As tensions rose with the increase in "scientific" bases, representatives from the twelve nations with stations in Antarctica convened in Washington in 1958 to address the future of the continent. While the territorial claims were not abandoned, they were suspended, leading to the signing of the Antarctic Treaty in 1959 and its enforcement in 1961.

As of today, nearly sixty countries have signed the Antarctic Treaty, which is set to expire in 2048. However, there is a consensus among the signatories to extend its validity for many more years beyond that.

The first meeting of the Antarctic Treaty Countries in July 1961 after the signing

British Icebreaker *HMS Protector*

Chilean station González Videla at Paradise Bay

The five main items of the Antarctic Treaty are:

1. Peaceful Purposes: Antarctica is to be used only for peaceful activities. Military actions, nuclear testing, and nuclear waste disposal are strictly prohibited.

2. Scientific Research: The treaty promotes freedom of scientific research, encouraging international collaboration, data sharing, and information exchange among nations.

3. Environmental Conservation: Parties to the treaty are committed to conserving the unique Antarctic environment, protecting its flora, fauna, and ecosystems. Special areas may be designated for environmental preservation.

4. Territorial Claims: The treaty suspends existing territorial claims and forbids any new claims, ensuring Antarctica remains a neutral and demilitarized continent.

5. International Cooperation: The treaty fosters cooperation through regular consultative meetings, information sharing, and consensus-based decision-making among signatory nations.

The original Antarctic Treaty, while not directly mentioning fishing, acknowledged the significance of preserving the marine living resources in the

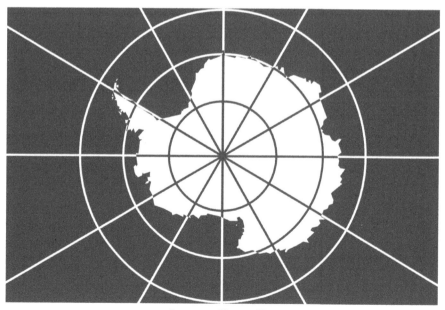

Antarctic Treaty Flag

Argentine summer stations are resupplied by conventional navy ships

Stonington Island's Historic site

Southern Ocean. To address fishing-related issues, the Commission for the Conservation of Antarctic Marine Living Resources (CCAMLR) was formed in 1982, operating within the framework of the treaty. CCAMLR's primary mission is to safeguard and sustainably manage the marine resources in the Antarctic region.

CCAMLR establishes fishing regulations, such as catch limits, area closures, and conservation measures, to prevent overfishing and safeguard the delicate Antarctic ecosystem. By doing so, CCAMLR plays a crucial role in ensuring the responsible and sustainable management of Antarctic marine resources for the benefit of present and future generations.

CCAMLR has taken significant steps to regulate the fishing of krill and whales in Antarctica, ensuring the protection and sustainability of these important species:

➤ Krill Fishing: CCAMLR sets catch limits and fishing regulations for krill to maintain a balanced krill population and preserve its crucial role in the Antarctic ecosystem. Scientific research guides the establishment of precautionary catch limits, and measures are implemented to safeguard krill predators, like whales and seals, by creating buffer zones around their feeding areas.

➤ Whale Protection: CCAMLR strictly enforces a comprehensive ban on the commercial hunting of whales in the Southern Ocean. Aligned with the International Whaling Commission's moratorium on commercial whaling, this ban provides essential protection to various whale species, ensuring they are not targeted or exploited.

Through these actions and standards, CCAMLR strives to maintain the ecological balance of the Antarctic marine environment, protect key species such as krill and whales, and ensure sustainable fishing practices that preserve the integrity and biodiversity of the region.

IAATO and Ecotourism

As we've discussed, the Antarctic environment is incredibly delicate. In addition to challenges like fishing and global warming, tourism can also have a negative impact. While many view tourism as a chance to raise awareness and funding for scientific research, it must be done responsibly to avoid harming the fragile ecosystem. Properly managed, tourism can be an opportunity, but it's crucial to minimize any negative environmental effects.

In 1991, the Antarctic Environmental Protocol was signed, going beyond the provisions of the 1959 Antarctic Treaty, and it set stricter standards for safeguarding the Antarctic environment. This protocol served as a crucial framework for ongoing protection efforts. At that time, seven companies that had been conducting expeditions to Antarctica for some time came together to establish the International Association of Antarctica Tour Operators (IAATO). IAATO is a global, non-profit organization that is committed to promoting safe and responsible private-sector travel to Antarctica.

IAATO is a voluntary organization that works closely with the Antarctic Treaty System. It aims to advance safe and environmentally responsible tourism in Antarctica while supporting the objectives of the Antarctic Treaty. The organization establishes guidelines and regulations for tour operators to ensure that visitor activities have minimal impacts on the environment and wildlife. IAATO collaborates with treaty parties, providing valuable information, data, and expertise to aid in the effective management and conservation of Antarctica. Though IAATO is not officially part of the treaty, its endeavors align with the treaty's mission of preserving Antarctica and fostering responsible human activities on the continent.

IAATO consists of various companies and entities that are committed to promoting responsible tourism in Antarctica. Today it has more than 100 members. While the specific members can change over time, some notable companies and entities that are of this organization include:

✓ Tour Operators and Expedition Cruise Lines such as: Abercrombie & Kent, Lindblad Expeditions, Quark Expeditions, G Adventures, Hurtigruten, Ponant, Silversea Expeditions, National Geographic Expeditions, Scenic Cruises and Oceanwide Expeditions to name a few.

✓ Research Institutions: Some scientific research institutions and organizations also participate in IAATO, contributing their expertise in the Antarctic region.

✓ Supportive Entities: Companies providing services and support to Antarctic expeditions, such as logistics, transportation, and infrastructure development, may also be members of IAATO.

The association aims to ensure that all member organizations adhere to the highest standards of safety, environmental stewardship, and responsible tourism practices in Antarctica.

IAATO establishes several guidelines and restrictions for landing places in Antarctica to ensure responsible tourism practices. Some of the main guidelines include:

➢ Site Protection: Identifies and designates landing sites to minimize environmental impact, taking into account factors like sensitive wildlife habitats, historical sites, and fragile ecosystems.

➢ Visitor Limits: Sets limits on the number of visitors that can land at a particular site simultaneously to prevent overcrowding and maintain a peaceful experience for both visitors and wildlife.

➢ Time Limits: Specifies time limits for visits to landing sites to prevent overexposure of the area and allow adequate rest and recovery time for wildlife.

➢ Biosecurity Measures: Enforces strict biosecurity protocols to prevent the introduction of non-native species or contaminants to the pristine Antarctic environment. These measures include cleaning and disinfection of equipment and mandatory visitor briefings.

➢ Wildlife Disturbance Avoidance: Instructs operators and visitors to maintain a safe distance from wildlife, respecting their natural behavior and avoiding any disturbance or harm.

➢ Waste Management: Mandates strict waste management practices, including the removal of all human-generated waste, following the principle of leaving no trace behind.

These guidelines and restrictions, among others, aim to protect the unique Antarctic environment, minimize human impacts, and ensure a sustainable and respectful experience for visitors while preserving the delicate balance of the ecosystem.

During the 2022-2023 austral season, over 105,000 tourists visited Antarctica. It's reassuring to know that IAATO diligently oversees the possible impact of tourism.

During your voyage, you may notice that some groups of scientists are also onboard the cruise ship. They are part of scientific studies promoted and supported by tour operators and cruise companies. These dedicated scientists often give lectures to passengers, sharing insights into their research and goals. We encourage you to attend these lectures as they can be both fascinating and educational, providing a deeper understanding of the wonders and importance of Antarctica's unique ecosystem. By learning from these experts, you'll gain a greater appreciation for the value of preserving and protecting this pristine continent for future generations.

It's wonderful to know that your trip offers more than just a chance to have a great time; it also plays a significant role in supporting and indirectly funding studies dedicated to preserving this pristine continent. So, as you embark on this remarkable adventure, you can take pride in knowing that your trip has a positive impact on the protection and understanding of this extraordinary part of our planet.

Chapter 5

Photography in Antarctica

Capturing photos, especially good ones, has become essential. Not only for sharing on social media but also to reminisce about the incredible journey once you return home. During an Antarctic trip, this becomes even more vital as your loved ones eagerly await your photos. Unlike European or US cities, revisiting Antarctica isn't easy, adding pressure to seize unforgettable moments with great pictures. It's a rare opportunity you wouldn't want to miss!

Usually, one person in a couple is a photo-perfectionist while the other isn't. In this scenario, we recommend that both of you try to capture beautiful images. It's not necessary for both to use SLR (Single Lens Reflex) cameras; one of you can use an SLR camera, while the other can use a good smartphone or a pocket camera. This way, you can both enjoy the photography experience without feeling overwhelmed.

Having an SLR camera will be beneficial for capturing distant shots of whales or wildlife. For simpler pictures, modern smartphones like the iPhone 13 or Samsung Ultra S23 are great options to obtain images with perfect lighting and focus. So, whether you have an SLR camera or a high-end smartphone, you'll have the tools to capture stunning images of the remarkable Antarctic wildlife.

Between SLR cameras and smartphones, there are pocket cameras that strike a balance. Our recommended choice is the Canon Powershot SX720 HS due to its compact size, lightweight design, user-friendly interface, and impressive 40X zoom capability. With this camera, you can effortlessly capture stunning images.

In photography, composition and seizing the moment matter more than having bulky and costly equipment. In fact, modern smartphones with their intelligent features and quality lenses often outperform traditional SLR cameras in many situations.

To enhance your smartphone photography experience, consider purchasing a phone grip or handle to reduce the risk of dropping your device during your trip. You can find various models for less than 15 dollars, ensuring both convenience and peace of mind.

Edition software – Photo editing software plays a crucial role in enhancing great photos, but it doesn't have to be complicated. We recommend using Snapseed, a user-friendly mobile app available for free download. With just a few filters, you can easily improve your pictures. Start by cropping the image to remove any unwanted parts. Adding a subtle HDR effect can enhance specific elements, particularly if there are clouds in the sky. Adjusting

saturation, contrast, and brightness will also yield excellent results. Additionally, you can lighten dark areas for further refinement.

Practice using this software (or any other that you may choose) before travelling.

Vertical or Horizontal? – In the past, we mainly captured horizontal photos, but with the rise of platforms like Instagram, vertical photos have become more popular for publications. The solution is simple: shoot the same picture in both horizontal and vertical formats. This way, you can choose the best one based on the publication's requirements. However, there are some guidelines to consider. If you want to showcase heights, or people, vertical photos work best. For landscapes, horizontal photos are more suitable. Ideally, capture both orientations to have more options – and it won't cost you anything!

Shoot many times the same situation – In the past, we used films that needed development, which incurred costs. But now, with digital photography, it's free! So, you can capture many shots of the same scene with various angles. For instance, try one from chest-height, another from head height, and a third by extending your arms or moving from left to right (or vice versa). Later, you can review and select the best shot at the end of the day. Digital photography offers this flexibility without worrying about developing expenses.

When taking pictures of people, aim to take at least three shots to ensure you get the best expressions. If there are multiple individuals involved, take more photos as there are greater chances of someone blinking, making funny faces, or having unexpected expressions. Taking multiple shots increases the likelihood of capturing those perfect moments.

Centering the target? "Rule of Thirds" – When taking photos, beginners often place the subject right in the center, but using the "Rule of Thirds" can lead to better results, especially in horizontal pictures. Imagine a picture divided into three columns and three rows. The main subjects of your photo should ideally be positioned where the numbers are. For instance, when capturing people's faces, they should be placed in positions 1 or 2, never looking out of

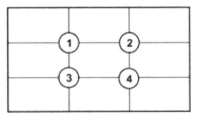

the frame. They can either face the camera directly (although not always necessary) or be at a 45-degree angle towards your right (if in position 1) or to your left (if in position 2), always looking towards the center of the photo. This technique can enhance the composition and overall appeal of your photos.

People, boats or animals should be facing/moving towards the center. Positions 1 and 3 pointing/moving to your right and positions 2 and 4 to the left.

Foreground & Background – Whenever you can, try to combine a foreground and a background in your photos. For instance, include a rock as the foreground and a striking mountain range as the background. This formula often creates visually appealing pictures. If the photo is vertical, align the background target directly above the foreground target. For horizontal photos, position the targets along a diagonal line. Using the "Rule of Thirds," if the foreground target is in position 3, place the background target in position 2 or vice versa; if the foreground is in position 4, place the background in position 1. This technique can add depth and interest to your photos, making them more captivating.

People – When taking pictures of people, ensure they are well-lit. Avoid capturing them wearing hats or caps that cast shadows over their faces. You can have them look at the camera (although not always) or integrate them into the surroundings. For instance, your spouse could be engaged in conversation with a guide instead of simply posing for the camera. Capturing candid moments and interactions can result in more authentic and captivating photographs. Remember, good lighting and natural expressions can make a significant difference in the overall quality of your people-centric photos.

Wildlife – Photographing animals with a smartphone can be challenging, as it might be hard to get close enough for a decent-sized shot, especially with whales or birds. In such situations, a Pocket camera with a 30x zoom or more, or a SLR camera with a 200 mm or 300 mm lens, will work better. Be patient, conceal your presence, and remain silent to avoid startling the animals. When photographing birds, it's best to avoid walking in large groups, as they may get scared away. By adopting these tips, you increase your chances of capturing stunning wildlife shots during your Antarctic journey.

Lines & Geometrical shapes – Our brains are naturally drawn to patterns, so incorporating these elements can enhance the composition. For example, a zodiac wake leading to a distant mountain creates a compelling visual path. Diagonal lines often create a sense of movement and dynamic energy, making them more effective than vertical lines in many compositions. Additionally, you can experiment with using the horizon as a leading line to guide the viewer's gaze through the image.

Reflections – Beautiful pictures can be achieved when you find a waveless sea. Surprisingly, you'll have these chances in Antarctica. Just be patient, and you might witness a perfect reflection before your eyes.

Epic landscapes – Antarctica offers epic landscapes that leave you speechless. Capturing that feeling in a photo is challenging, but you can try by adding a friend or spouse with an "awe-inspired" expression, gazing at the landscape. They can appear small or medium-sized, not central to the photo. Place them using the Rule of Thirds. A bright jacket or backpack will make them stand out. Luckily, most cruise companies provide colorful jackets.

Distance & Relative Sizes – You can create interesting effects by playing with the distance between the foreground (a person) and a large object in the background (a mountain or the moon). How? When you are very near the foreground object, this one will appear to be bigger than that of the background and vice versa if you retreat far from foreground object. Many times, you'll have to compensate distance with the zoom. Check the drawing below the 3 situations. In Position 1 the foreground A appears smaller than the background object B. If you approach (move to P2) you'll eventually succeed in having foreground with the same apparent size as the background. If you approach even more (P3) you'll have the foreground object apparently bigger than the background. To achieve these effects, you may need to use the zoom function. Experiment with different distances and zoom levels to get creative shots.

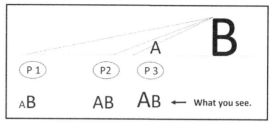

Light – The sun will be your ally when you have it behind you and your enemy if it faces you. It's almost impossible to take a great picture with the sun shining behind your target. If its people, you can move them around but if your target is a mountain you might have to rely on your smartphone or edition software to improve the light.

Backup of your photos – How can you download/backup your smartphone photos to your computer? Easy.

• IOS - If you have an Iphone - your mobile will upload the picture to iCloud. When you arrive home from your (fantastic) trip you can access iCloud using your computer (www.icloud.com) with your apple user and password. There you can download to your computer using date filters or folders. Before your starting your trip check that your iCloud does have enough available space (20Gb should do), if not, but extra space.

• Android – Similarly, if you have Android mobile phone you should download the Google Photos App. This will automatically backup your photos in Google's cloud. Back home you can access https://photos.google.com with your Google user and password and Bingo! The photos are there! Then you can simply choose the pictures (by date) that you want to download to your computer.

Instagram & Facebook – It would be nice if, when you upload your photos to your social networks, you use the hashtag #BeThereGuide so that we can see your picture and comment them. Thank you!

PHOTOGRAPHIC GUIDE OF PATAGONIA

BE THERE

200 GREAT PICTURES THAT YOU CAN TAKE WITH YOUR SMARTPHONE OR POCKET CAMERA

PAULA FORD - GERARDO BARTOLOMÉ

Chapter 6

Ideas and Combinations of Antarctica with Other Destinations

A trip to Antarctica involves two flights: a long one to Buenos Aires or Santiago and a shorter one to Ushuaia or Punta Arenas/Puerto Williams, the Southern tip of South America. You'll need four navigation days (two going and two returning) to spend a week among the ice. In total, the trip takes at least two weeks, including flights.

Some travelers feel that such an long journey deserves more time, and they wonder what else they can do in the region. Here are some ideas and comments:

Buenos Aires – At least 2 days – This is the obvious alternative. The capital of Argentina is full of interesting things to see and do. Shopping, tango dancing, gaucho barbecue, architecture, cool restaurants and a lot more... Even if you don't want to spend money on top of your Antarctica trip you should (must!) book at least two full days here. We are  now writing a guide about Buenos Aires so very soon you'll have a lot more information about this destination. If you're going to Antarctica through Chile, then you should book two days in Santiago.

Other places in Central and Northern Argentina – 2 or 3 days additional to your stay in Buenos Aires- Argentina has many amazing places to visit. Our recommendation is that you consider spending at least 2 weeks in Argentina, but we understand if you prefer to add just a few more days to your Antarctic adventure. In that case, we recommend choosing one of these alternatives:

➢ Iguazú falls – An incredible place! Fly and spend two days there. You won't regret it.
➢ Mendoza wine country – Two full days visiting vineyards at the foot of the Andes.
➢ Jujuy – Visit small villages with Inca heritage. You'll need at least three days there.

Chile – If you're going to Antarctica through Chile and want to spend an extra three days (besides two in Santiago), we recommend visiting San Pedro de Atacama, which includes an incredible geyser in the desert!

Malvinas/Falkland Islands and or South Georgia – These are fascinating destinations that some Antarctic cruise companies offer in addition to their Antarctica trips. However, it's essential to note that these extensions can be very expensive. Including these islands in your trip would require an additional 3 to 5 navigation days (going and returning) plus 2 to 3 days on the islands. Considering a cost of approximately 800 US

Dollars per day per person the additional cost of visiting these islands can range from around 8,000 to 12,000 US Dollars or Euros per couple over the cost of a "plain" Antarctica cruise. These options can be worthwhile for those looking for a more comprehensive Antarctic experience, but it's essential to consider the added expenses.

Ushuaia – 2 to 3 days – Ushuaia is a great option after your Antarctic trip. It's convenient and budget-friendly since it doesn't require extra flights or navigation days. You can spend 2 to 3 nights exploring the beautiful city and its surroundings. Ushuaia offers various activities such as easy trekking, breathtaking landscapes, historical tours, rainforests, and abundant flora

and fauna. Despite the short duration, you can have a fulfilling experience and make the most of your time in this unique location.

Southern Patagonia – 1 week – A fantastic alternative. In just one week, you can explore the breathtaking regions of Ushuaia and El Calafate. If you have ten days, consider adding Torres del Paine or El Chalten to your itinerary for an even more amazing experience. Whether you're starting your Antarctic journey

from Ushuaia or Punta Arenas, you can easily visit these stunning Patagonian destinations. For more details about these places, don't forget to check out our "Patagonia Travel Guide."

Travelling through Chile? consider spending three days exploring Punta Arenas and Torres del Paine, followed by two days in Santiago.

What we strongly suggest is considering adding a couple of destinations to your Antarctic adventure. The easiest and most affordable option is to spend 2 to 3 days in Ushuaia after your Antarctic journey, followed by 2 days in Buenos Aires before returning home. This way, you get the chance to explore more of Argentina's beautiful landscapes and vibrant culture, making your trip even more memorable and fulfilling. Ushuaia offers breathtaking natural wonders, while Buenos Aires presents a unique blend of history, art, and culinary delights. It's the perfect way to extend your experience and create lasting memories of your Antarctic expedition.

Feel free to send us an email to consultas@EdicionesHistoricas.com.ar with questions or ideas. We'll be more than glad to help you.

Appendix 1

Expedition Cruises Companies

These are the Expedition Cruise Companies (with landings):

➢ Antarctica 21 – www.Antartica21.com
➢ Atlas Ocean Voyages – www.AtlasOceanVoyages.com
➢ Aurora Expeditions – www.AuroraExpeditions.com.au
➢ Hapag-Lloyd Cruises – www.HL-Cruises.com
➢ Hurtigruten – www.Hurtigruten.com
➢ Lindblad Expeditions – www.LindbladCruises.com
➢ Oceanwide Expeditions – www.Oceanwide-Expeditions.com
➢ Ponant – www.Ponant.com
➢ Quark Expeditions – www.QuarkExpeditions.com
➢ Scenic – www.Scenic.co.uk
➢ Seabourn – www.Seabourn.com
➢ Silversea Expeditions – www.Silversea.com
➢ Swoop Antarctica – www.Swoop-Antarctica.com
➢ Viking – www.VikingCruises.com

Some tour operators, such as Adventures by Disney, Tauck, Abercrombie & Kent and Albatros Expeditions, charter vessels for the Antarctica itineraries.

Check the updated list of licensed vessels:

https://iaato.org/who-we-are/vessel-directory/

The following links may help you to compare:

https://wayfinderadventures.com/

https://freestyleadventuretravel.com/all-trips/?fwp_destination=antarctic

Appendix 2

List of Landing Sites

IAATO Peninsula Map Overview (Courtesy IAATO)

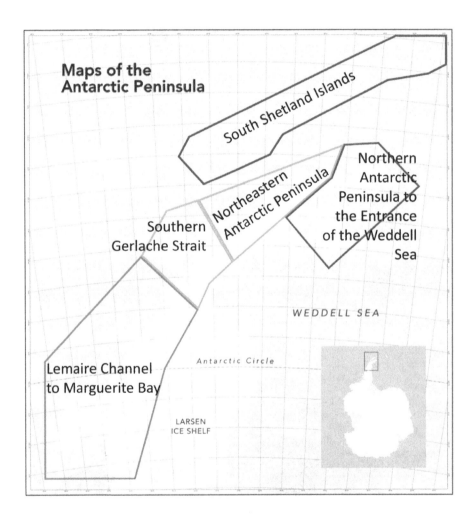

Maps of the
Antarctic Peninsula

South Shetland Islands

Northeastern
Antarctic Peninsula

Northern
Antarctic
Peninsula to
the Entrance
of the Weddell
Sea

Southern
Gerlache Strait

WEDDELL SEA

Lemaire Channel
to Marguerite Bay

Antarctic Circle

LARSEN
ICE SHELF

South Shetland Islands

1 Smith Island	19 Fort Point	37 Aspland Island
2 Low Island	20 Barrientos Island - Aitcho Islands	38 Gibbs Island
3 Boyd Strait	21 English Strait	39 Cape Lookout
4 Snow Island	22 Robert Island	40 Elephant Island
5 President Head	23 Robert Point	41 Point Wild
6 Elephant Point	24 Bransfield Strait	42 Cape Valentine
7 Walker Bay	25 Nelson Strait	43 Cornwallis Island
8 Hannah Point	26 Nelson Island	44 Clarence Island
9 Livingston Island	27 Ardley Island	45 North Foreland
10 Half Moon Island	28 Great Wall Station - China	46 Cape Melville
11 Deception Island	29 Frei Station - Chile	47 Ferraz Station - Brazil
12 Telefon Bay	30 Bellingshausen Station - Russia	48 Machu Picchu Staion - Peru
13 Pendulum Cove	31 Artigas Station - Uruguay	49 Admiralty Bay
14 Vapor Colony	32 Jubany Station - Argentina	50 Lions Rump
15 Whaler's Bay	33 Arctowski Station - Poland	51 Marsh Station - Chile
16 Baily Head	34 King George Island	52 Potter Cove
17 Greenwich Island	35 Turret Point	53 Maxwell Bay
18 Yankee Harbour	36 Penquin Island	54 Port Foster

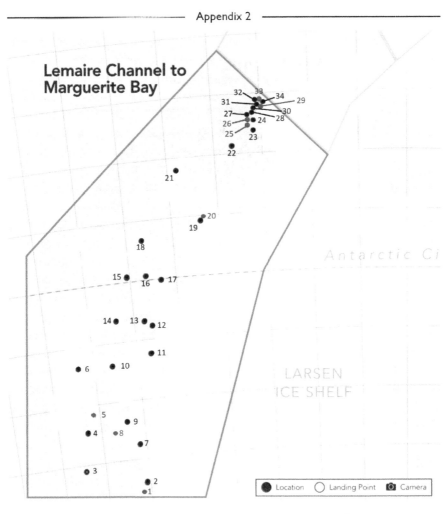

Lemaire Channel to Marguerite Bay

Legend: ● Location ○ Landing Point 📷 Camera

1	Red Rock Ridge	14	Liard Island	27	French Passage
2	Stonington Island	15	Barcroft Islands	📷 28	Petermann Island
3	Marguerite Bay	16	Crystal Sound	29	Penola Strait
4	Jenny Island	17	Antarctic Circle	30	Hovgaard Island
5	Rothera Station - UK	18	Lavoisier Island	31	Pleneau Island
6	Adelaide Island	19	Fish Islands	32	Iceberg Alley
7	Horseshoe Island	20	Prospect Point	33	Port Charcot
8	Bongrain Point	21	Renaud Island	34	Lemaire Channel
9	Pourquois Pas Island	22	Grandidier Channel	35	Pitt Islands
10	The Gullet	23	Berthelot Islands	36	Adie Cove
11	Lallemand Fjord	📷 24	Yalour Islands	37	IAATO Islands
12	Andresen Island	25	Wordie House	38	Skog Bay
13	Detaille island	26	Vernadsky Station - Ukraine		

Southern
Gerlache Strait

Location   Landing Point   Camera

1	Anvers Island	19	Ronge Island	📷 35	Goudier Island - Port Lockroy
2	Fournier Bay	20	Ketley Point	📷 36	Damoy Point/Dorian Bay
3	Dallmann Bay	21	Useful Islands	📷 37	Jougla Point
4	Melchior Islands	📷 22	Cuverville Island	38	Doumer Island
5	Brabant Island	📷 23	Danco Island	39	Yelcho Station - Chile
6	Charlotte Bay	24	Beneden Head	40	Lion Sound
7	Portal Point	25	Andvord Bay	41	Neumayer Channel
8	Enterprise Islands	📷 26	Neko Harbour	42	Palmer Station - USA
9	Foyn Harbour	27	Waterboat Point	43	Bismarck Starit
10	Nansen Islands		Gabriel Gonzales Videla Station	44	Cape Renard
11	Wilhelmina Bay		- Chile	45	Hidden Bay
12	Gerlache Strait	28	Lemaire Island	46	Flanders Bay
13	Errera Channel	29	Paradise Harbour	47	Borgen Bay
14	Spigot Peak	30	Bryde Island	48	Peltier Channel
📷 15	Orne Harbour	31	Brown Station - Argentina	49	Ferguson Channel
16	Orne Islands	32	Skontorp Cove	50	Leith Cove
📷 17	Georges Point	33	Stony Point	51	Plata Passage
18	Kerr Point	34	Weinke Island		

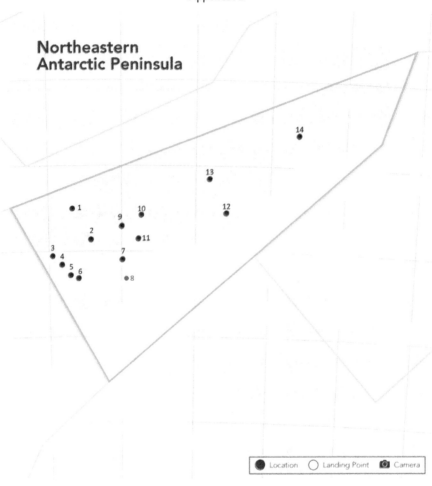

Northeastern Antarctic Peninsula

1	Hoseason Island	6	Hydruga Rocks	11	Mikkelsen Harbour
2	Intercurrence Island	7	Cierva Cove	12	Charcot Bay
3	Liege Island	8	Primivera Station - Argentina	13	Tower Island
4	Croker Passage	9	Spert Island	14	Astrolabe Island
5	Two Hummock Island	10	Trinity Island	15	Lindblad Cove

Location   Landing Point   Camera

Northern Antarctic Peninsula to the Entrance of the Weddell Sea

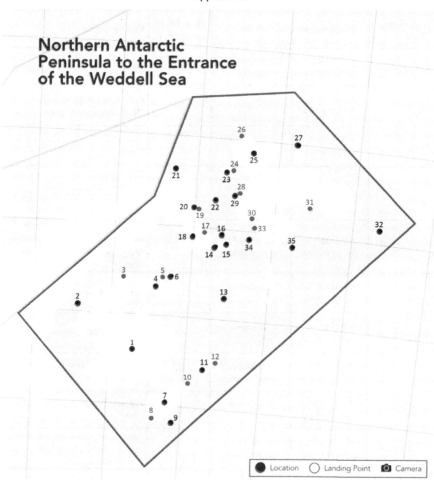

| | Location | ◯ Landing Point | 📷 Camera |

1 James Ross Island
2 Prince Gustav Channel
3 Mendel Station - Czech Republic
4 Vega Island
5 Cape Wellmet
6 Devil Island
7 Snow Hill Island
8 Snow Hill Emperor Penguin Colony
9 Snow Hill Ice Edge (Varies from Year to Year)
10 Snow Hill - Nordenskjold's Hut
11 Seymour Island
12 Marambio Station - Argentina

13 Erebus and Terror Gulf
14 Fridtjof Sound
15 Andersson Island
16 Jonassen Island
📷 17 Brown Bluff
18 Tabarin Peninsula
19 Esperanza Station - Argentina
20 Hope Bay
21 Gourdin Island
22 Antarctic Sound
23 Bransfield Island
24 Knobble Head
25 D'Urville Island
26 Cape Juncal

27 Wideopen Islands
28 Madder Cliffs
29 Kinnes Cove
30 D'Urville Monument
31 Tay Head
32 Danger Islands
33 Petrel Station - Argentina
34 Rosamel Island
35 Paulet Island
36 Larsen Channel
37 Joinville Island
38 Active Sound
39 Dundee Island

Landing Site	Coordinates	Area	Max. N° of passengers	Key Features
Ardley Island	62°12'00''S, 58°55'00''W	South Shetland Islands	20	Gentoo and Adelie penguins
Astrolabe Island	63°17'00''S, 58°40'00''W	Northeastern Antarctic Peninsula	100	Chinstrap penguins. Crescent Moon shaped long gravelly beach
Baily Head, Deception Island	62°58'00''S, 60°30'00''W	South Shetland Islands	100	Chinstrap Penguins. Outstanding Scenery
Barrientos Island	62°24'00''S, 59°47'00''W	South Shetland Islands	100	Gentoo and Chinstrap Penguins. Southern Elephant Seals. Geological features. Southern Giant Petrels
Brown Bluff	63°32'00''S, 56°52'00''W	Northern Ant. Pen & Weddell	100	Geological features including towering red brown cliffs Adélie and gentoo penguins. Continental landing
Cuverville Island	64°41'00''S, 62°38'00''W	Southern Gerlache Strait	100	Extensive colony of Gentoo penguins. Glacial and ice scenery. Whaling artefacts
Damoy Point	64°49'00''S, 63°30'00''W	Southern Gerlache Strait	100	Historic British and Argentine field huts. Gentoo penguin colony. Glacial scenery
Danco Island	64°44'00''S, 62°36'00''W	Southern Gerlache Strait	100	Gentoo penguin colony. Glacial scenery
Detaille Island	66°52'00''S, 66°48'00''W	Lemaire & Marguerite Bay	50	Historic British Base 'W', Detaille Island
Devil Island	63°48'00''S, 57°17'00''W	Northern Ant. Pen & Weddell	100	Adélie penguins, two summits, volcanic rock face, scenic views on the upper peak
D'Hainaut Island	63°54'00''S, 60°47'00''W	Northeastern Antarctic Peninsula	100	Gentoo Penguins. Whaling Artefacts. Argentine Refuge
George's Point, Rongé Island	64°40'00''S, 62°40'00''W	Southern Gerlache Strait	100	Gentoo penguins, with chinstraps also present. Glacial and ice scenery
Goudier Island - Port Lockroy	64°49'00''S, 63°29'00''W	Southern Gerlache Strait	60	Historic British Base A, Port Lockroy. Gentoo Penguins. Glacial Scenery
Half Moon Island	62°35'24''S, 59°55'13''W	South Shetland Islands	100	Chinstrap penguins. Vegetation. Wilson's storm-petrels. Weddell & fur seal haul-out
Hannah Point	62°39'00''S, 60°37'00''W	South Shetland Islands	100	High concentration of diverse wildlife: nesting gentoo, chinstrap, and a small number of macaroni penguins; nesting southern giant petrels; southern elephant seals

Landing Site	Coordinates	Area	Max. N° of passengers	Key Features
Horseshoe Island	67°49'00''S, 67°18'00''W	Lemaire & Marguerite Bay	100	Historic British Base 'Y'
Jougla Point	64°50'00''S, 63°29'00''W	Southern Gerlache Strait	100	Gentoo penguins. Blue-eyed shags. Glacial scenery. Whale bones
Neko Harbour	64°51'00''S, 62°32'00''W	Southern Gerlache Strait	100	Glacial scenery. Gentoo Penguins. Continental landing
Orne Harbour	64°38'00''S, 62°33'00''W	Southern Gerlache Strait	100	Chinstrap penguin colonies, Blue-eyed shag colony, Viewpoint
Orne Islands	64°40'00''S, 62°40'00''W	Southern Gerlache Strait	100	Outstanding views of Gerlache Strait, Errera Channel and Cuverville Island. Chinstrap and Gentoo penguin colonies
Paulet Island	63°35'00''S, 55°47'00''W	Northern Ant. Pen & Weddell	100	Extensive Adélie Penguin colony. Stone hut, grave and cairn (Historic Site and Monument N°. 41). Outstanding volcanic scenery
Pendulum Cove, Deception Island	62°56'00''S, 60°36'00''W	South Shetland Islands	100	Geothermally Heated Water. Historic Site
Penguin Island	62°06'00''S, 57°54'00''W	South Shetland Islands	100	Dormant volcanic cone. Southern Giant Petrels. Chinstrap Penguins. Vegetation. Whale bone
Petermann Island	65°10'00''S, 64°08'00''W	Lemaire & Marguerite Bay	100	Gentoo and Adélie Penguins. Blue-eyed Shags. Mountainous Scenery. Site of Charcot's second French Antarctic expedition. Cairn and Commemorative Cros
Pleneau Island	65°06'00''S, 64°04'00''W	Lemaire & Marguerite Bay	100	Iceberg and glacial scenery. Gentoo penguins. Glacially smoothed rock terraces
Point Wild, Elephant Island	61°06'00''S, 54°52'00''W	South Shetland Islands	30	Chinstrap penguin colony, mosses & lichens. Site of Sir Ernest Shackleton's shipwrecked Endurance expedition
Port Charcot	65°04'00''S, 64°02'00''W	Lemaire & Marguerite Bay	100	Historic site of Charcot's 1st French Antarctic Expedition (HSM 28). All three pygoscelid species of penguins nest on the island. Glacial scenery
Portal Point	64°30'00''S, 61°46'00''W	Southern Gerlache Strait	100	Accessible glacier walk and glacial scenery. Continental landing site

Landing Site	Coordinates	Area	Max. N° of passengers	Key Features
Shingle Cove	60°39'00''S, 45°34'00''W	Northern Ant. Pen & Weddell	100	Adélie penguins. Vegetation. Burrowing snow petrels
Snow Hill Hut	64°21'50''S, 56°59'31''W	Northern Ant. Pen & Weddell	100	Wooden hut of the expedition led by Otto Nordenskjöld (1902). Presence of basalt dikes
Stonington Island	68°11'00''S, 67°00'00''W	Lemaire & Marguerite Bay	100	Historic East Base (USA). Historic Base 'E' Stonington (UK), including the graves of Noel and Allen. Glacial scenery
Telefon Bay, Deception Island	62°56'00''S, 60°40'00''W	South Shetland Islands	100	Volcanic Crater. Outstanding scenery
Turret Point	62°05'00''S, 57°55'00''W	South Shetland Islands	100	Southern Giant Petrels. Blue-eyed Shags. Chinstrap and Adélie Penguins. Southern Elephant Seals
Whalers Bay, Deception Island	62°59'00''S, 60°34'00''W	South Shetland Islands	100	Historic site, remains of the Norwegian Hektor Whaling Station, Whaler's Cemetery, abandoned British 'Base B'
Wordie House	65°15'00''S, 64°16'00''W	Lemaire & Marguerite Bay	36	Historic British Base 'F', Wordie House. Glacial scenery
Yalour Islands	65°14'00''S, 64°10'00''W	Lemaire & Marguerite Bay	60	Adélie penguin colony and one of the southernmost recorded gentoo penguin colonies. Summer habitat of orcas foraging on penguins and seals
Yankee Harcour	62°32'00''S, 59°47'00''W	South Shetland Islands	100	Gentoo penguins (several thousand), A trypot and the foundation of a sealer's hut on the inner shoreline. Whale bones
Heroina Island	63°24'S 54°36'W	Northern Ant. Pen & Weddell	20	Adélie penguin colony and 8 other birds breeding sites
President Head	62°44'0''S, 061°12'33''W	South Shetland Islands	100	Elephant seals, chinstrap penguins, southern giant petrels and Antarctic terns
Red Rock Ridge	68° 20.9208' S, 67° 05.8890' W	Lemaire & Marguerite Bay	100	Adelie penguin colony. Continental landing. Dramatic landscape
Elephant Point	62° 41'32.7S 60°51' 26.4W	South Shetland Islands	100	Elephant Seals. Southern Giant Petrels, Sealer remains

Appendix 3

General Behaviour Guidelines for Visitors to Antarctica

These guidelines apply to all visitors and all activities in the Antarctic Treaty area providing general guidance for visiting any location, with the aim of ensuring that visits do not have adverse impacts on the Antarctic environment, including wildlife and ecosystems, or on its scientific, wilderness and aesthetic values. If you are part of a guided visitor group, abide by these guidelines, pay attention to your guides, and follow their instructions.

Protect Antarctic Wildlife

- The taking of, or harmful interference with, Antarctic wildlife is prohibited.
- When in the vicinity of wildlife, either on land or at sea, move or maneuver slowly and carefully and keep noise to a minimum.
- Maintain an appropriate distance from wildlife to avoid disturbance. While in many cases a greater distance may be necessary, in general keep at least 5 m from wildlife on land. Abide by any guidance on distances in species or site-specific guidelines.
- Always give animals the right of way and do not block their access routes between the sea and land, nesting places or other destinations.
- Animals may alter their behavior if disturbed. Observe wildlife behaviour. If wildlife changes its behaviour (standing when it was sitting, moving

its head around alerted, start vocalizing when it was silent, etc.) stop moving, or slowly increase your distance.
• Stay outside the margins of a colony and observe from a safe distance. Animals are particularly sensitive to disturbance when they are breeding (including nesting) or moulting.
• Every situation is different. Consider the topography and the individual circumstances of the site, as these may have an impact on the vulnerability of wildlife to disturbance.
• Watch your steps for eggs, chicks or nest materials of skuas, penguins or petrels.
• Do not feed wildlife or leave food or scraps lying around.

Protecting Antarctic Vegetation

• Vegetation, including mosses and lichens, is fragile and very slow growing. Do not walk, drive or land on any moss beds or lichen covered rocks, in order to avoid damage.

- When travelling on foot, stay on established tracks whenever possible to minimize disturbance or damage to the soil and vegetated surfaces. Where a track does not exist, choose your route carefully, taking the most direct route while avoiding vegetation, fragile terrain, scree slopes, and wildlife.

Introduction of Non-Native Species and Pathogens

- Do not introduce any plants or animals into the Antarctic.
- In order to prevent the introduction of non-native species and disease, carefully wash boots and clean all equipment including clothes, bags, tripods, tents and walking sticks before bringing them to Antarctica. Pay particular attention to boot treads, velcro fastenings and pockets which could contain soil or seeds. Vehicles and aircraft should also be cleaned.
- In order to prevent the transfer of non-native species and disease between locations in Antarctica ensure all clothing, boots and equipment are cleaned thoroughly before moving between sites and regions.

Historic Sites, Monuments and Other Structures

Historic huts and structures can, in some cases, be visited for touristic, recreational and educational purposes. Visitors should not use them for other purposes except in emergency circumstances.

Do not damage, remove, destroy or change any historic site, monument, or artefact, or other building or emergency refuge (whether occupied or unoccupied).

Before entering any historic structure, clean your boots of snow and grit and remove snow and water from clothes, as these can cause damage to structures or artefacts.

Take care not to tread on any artefacts which may be obscured by sediments or snow when moving around historic sites.

If you come across an item that may be of historic value that authorities may not be aware of, do not touch or disturb it. Notify your expedition leader.

Respect of Scientific Research

Some Antarctic stations may accept visitors where prior arrangements have been made.

Do not interfere with or remove scientific equipment or markers, and do not disturb experimental study sites, field camps or stored supplies.

Keeping Antarctica Pristine by Leaving No Trace of Your Visit

• Do not deposit any litter or garbage on land nor discard it into the sea.
• No smoking except in designated areas at stations or camps, to avoid litter and risk of fire to structures. Collect ash and litter for disposal outside Antarctica.
• Ensure that all belongings, equipment and waste is secured at all times in such a way as to prevent dispersal into the environment through high winds or wildlife foraging.

Wilderness Values

• Do not disturb or pollute lakes, streams, rivers or other water bodies (e.g. by walking, washing yourself or your equipment, throwing stones, etc.)
• Do not paint or engrave names or other graffiti on any man-made or natural surface in Antarctica.
• Do not take souvenirs, whether man-made, biological or geological items, including feathers, bones, eggs, vegetation, soil, rocks, meteorites or fossils.
• Place tents and equipment on snow or at previously used campsites where possible.

Safety Precautions

• Be prepared for severe and changeable weather. Ensure that your equipment and clothing meet Antarctic standards. Remember that the Antarctic environment is inhospitable, unpredictable, and potentially dangerous.

- Know your capabilities, the dangers posed by the Antarctic environment, and act accordingly. Always act with safety in mind.
- Keep a larger safety distance from potentially dangerous or territorial wildlife like fur seals, both on land and at sea. Keep at least 15-25 m away where practicable.
- Be careful where you walk as seals can lie camouflaged on and among rocks. Keep a safety distance from sea-ice edge and be cautious when stepping over cracks in the sea ice.
- Skuas are very territorial birds and will attack anyone approaching their nests by plummeting down on intruders. If this happens, retreat away from the point when the attack started.
- Any wildlife, even penguins, can cause serious harm. Do not underestimate risks.
- Act on the guidance and instructions of your leaders. Do not stray from your group as survival in Antarctica can be a matter of minutes (especially in case of acute hypothermia).
- Do not walk onto glaciers or large snow fields. There is a real danger of falling into hidden crevasses.
- Be vigilant in the vicinity of calving glaciers. Breaking pieces of ice can generate dangerous waves.
- Pay special attention when climbing rocks and/or boulders, as melting permafrost with changing temperatures lead to an increased risk of avalanches.
- Do not expect a rescue service. Self-sufficiency is increased and risks reduced by sound planning, quality equipment, and trained personnel.
- Enter emergency refuges only in case of an actual emergency. If you use equipment or food from a refuge, inform the nearest research station or the National Competent Authority that has approved/permitted the visitors activity in Antarctica once the emergency is over.
- Respect every fire restriction. Use of combustion style lanterns and naked flames in or around historic structures is strictly discouraged. Take great care to safeguard against the danger of fire. This is a real hazard in the dry environment of Antarctica.

Argentina's Brown station stands at the foot of a glacier

Appendix 4

List of Antarctic Stations

Name	Location	Country	Status	Year est.	Summer pop.	Winter pop.
Marambio	Marambio Island	Argentina	Permanent	1969	165	70
Esperanza	Hope Bay	Argentina	Permanent	1953	116	56
Carlini	King George Island	Argentina	Permanent	1953	80	29
Orcadas	Laurie Island, South Orkney Islands	Argentina	Permanent	1903	35	17
San Martín	Barry Island	Argentina	Permanent	1951	19	21
Belgrano II	Coats Land	Argentina	Permanent	1979	24	19
Petrel	Dundee Island	Argentina	Summer only	1967	25	
Deception	Deception Island	Argentina	Summer only	1948	18	
Cámara	Half Moon Island	Argentina	Summer only	1953	20	
Primavera	Graham Land	Argentina	Summer only	1977	18	
Melchior	Melchior Islands	Argentina	Summer only	1947	12	
Brown	Paradise Harbor	Argentina	Summer only	1951	12	
Matienzo	Graham Land	Argentina	Summer only	1961	12	
Casey	Vincennes Bay	Australia	Permanent	1957	99	21
Davis	Princess Elizabeth Land	Australia	Permanent	1957	91	17
Mawson	Mac Robertson Land	Australia	Permanent	1954	53	15
Vechernyaya	Mount Vechernyaya, Thala Hills	Belarus	Summer only	2007	11	
Princess Elisabeth	Queen Maud Land	Belgium	Summer only	2007	22	
Comandante Ferraz	King George Island	Brazil	Permanent	1984	35	15
St. Kliment Ohridski	Emona Anchorage, Livingston Island	Bulgaria	Summer only	1988	22	
Eduardo Frei and Villa Las Estrellas	King George Island	Chile	Permanent	1969	150	80
Escudero	King George Island	Chile	Permanent	1995	60	2
General Bernardo O'Higgins	Cape Legoupil	Chile	Permanent	1948	52	24
Arturo Prat	Greenwich Island	Chile	Permanent	1947	30	8
Carvajal	Adelaide Island	Chile	Summer only	1984	46	
Yelcho	South Bay, Doumer Island	Chile	Summer only	1962	28	
González Videla	Waterboat Point, Graham Land	Chile	Summer only	1951	15	
Guillermo Mann	Cape Shirreff	Chile	Summer only	1991	8	

Name	Location	Country	Status	Year est.	Summer pop.	Winter pop.
Collins	Fildes Peninsula	Chile	Summer only	2006	6	
Julio Ripamonti	Ardley Island	Chile	Summer only	1982	4	
Risopatrón	Robert Island	Chile	Summer only	1949	6	
Union Glacier	Union Glacier	Chile	Summer only	2014	70	
Great Wall	King George Island	China	Permanent	1985	60	13
Zhongshan	Larsemann Hills, Prydz Bay	China	Permanent	1989	60	17
Kunlun	Dome A	China	Summer only	2009	26	
Taishan	Princess Elizabeth Land	China	Summer only	2014	20	
Eco-Nelson	Nelson Island	Czech Republic	Permanent	1988	5	5
Mendel	James Ross Island	Czech Republic	Summer only	2007	20	
Maldonado	Greenwich Island	Ecuador	Summer only	1990	32	
Aboa	Queen Maud Land	Finland	Summer only	1988	13	
Dumont d'Urville	Adélie Land	France	Permanent	1956	90	24
Neumayer III	Atka Bay	Germany	Permanent	2009	60	9
GARS	Cape Legoupil	Germany	Permanent	1991		
Kohnen	Queen Maud Land	Germany	Summer only	2001	6	
Dallmann	Carlini Station	Germany	Summer only	1994	16	
Gondwana	Transantarctic Mountains	Germany	Summer only	1983		
Maitri	Schirmacher Oasis	India	Permanent	1989	45	25
Bharati	Larsemann Hills	India	Permanent	2012	46	23
Zucchelli	Terra Nova Bay	Italy	Summer only	1986	120	
Concordia	Dome C, Antarctic Plateau	Italy/France	Permanent	2005	70	13
Showa	East Ongul Island	Japan	Permanent	1957	170	40
Dirck Gerritsz Laboratory	Rothera Station	Netherlands	Summer only	2013	10	
Scott Base	Ross Island	New Zealand	Permanent	1957	78	11
Arrival Heights Laboratory	Ross Island	New Zealand	Permanent	1959		
Troll	Queen Maud Land	Norway	Permanent	1990	45	7
Tor	Queen Maud Land	Norway	Summer only	1993	7	

Name	Location	Country	Status	Year est.	Summer pop.	Winter pop.
Jinnah	Sør Rondane Mountains, Queen Maud Land	Pakistan	Summer only	1991		
Machu Picchu	Admiralty Bay, King George Island	Peru	Summer only	1989	30	
Arctowski	King George Island	Poland	Permanent	1977	40	16
Dobrowolski	Bunger Hills, Wilkes Land	Poland	Summer only	1956	10	
Law-Racoviță-Negoiță	Larsemann Hills, Princess Elizabeth Land	Romania	Summer only	1986	13	
Novolaza-revskaya	Queen Maud Land	Russia	Permanent	1961	70	40
Mirny	Davis Sea	Russia	Permanent	1956	50	25
Progress	Prydz Bay	Russia	Permanent	1988	50	25
Bellingshau-sen	King George Island	Russia	Permanent	1968	40	20
Vostok	Antarctic Ice Sheet	Russia	Permanent	1957	30	15
Molodyozh-naya	Thala Hills, East Antarctica	Russia	Summer only	1962	15	
SANAE IV	Vesleskarvet, Queen Maud Land	South Africa	Permanent	1997	110	15
King Sejong	King George Island	South Korea	Permanent	1988	68	22
Jang Bogo	Terra Nova Bay	South Korea	Permanent	2014	62	23
Juan Carlos I	South Bay, Livingston Island	Spain	Summer only	1988	27	
Gabriel de Castilla	Deception Island	Spain	Summer only	1989	33	
Wasa	Queen Maud Land	Sweden	Summer only	1989	13	
Svea	Queen Maud Land	Sweden	Summer only	1988	5	
TARS	Horseshoe Island	Turkey	Summer only	2019	26	
Vernadsky	Galindez Island	Ukraine	Permanent	1994	30	12
Rothera	Adelaide Island	United Kingdom	Permanent	1975	160	27
Halley	Brunt Ice Shelf	United Kingdom	Permanent	2013	70	17
Signy [20]	Signy Island, South Orkney Islands	United Kingdom	Summer only	1947	14	
Port Lockroy	Goudier Island	United Kingdom	Summer only	1944	4	
McMurdo	Ross Island	United States	Permanent	1956	1,000	153

Name	Location	Country	Status	Year est.	Summer pop.	Winter pop.
Amundsen–Scott South Pole	Geographical South Pole	United States	Permanent	1957	150	49
Palmer	Anvers Island	United States	Permanent	1968	44	13
Lenie	Admiralty Bay	United States	Summer only	1985	2	
Shirreff	Cape Shirreff	United States	Summer only	1996	6	
Artigas	King George Island	Uruguay	Permanent	1984	9	8
Elichiribe-hety	Hope Bay	Uruguay	Summer only	1945	7	

A Gentoo penguin rookery around an old Argentina refuge hut

Appendix 5

List of Animals

This is a comprehensive list of animals that can be found in Antarctica, although some of them are not frequently observed in the region.

Whales

- Humpback whale
- Antarctic Minke whale
- Common minke whale
- Dwarf Minke whale
- Blue whale
- Fin whale
- Bryde's whale
- Sei whale
- Southern Right whale
- Sperm whale

Dolphins

- Orca / Killer whale
- Long-finned Pilot Whale

Seals and Sea Lions and Elephant Seals

- Antarctic Fur Seal
- Crabeater Seal
- Leopard Seal
- Weddell Seal
- Ross Seal
- Southern Elephant Seal

Penguins

- Chinstrap Penguin
- Gentoo Penguin
- Adelie Penguin
- Emperor Penguin

Birds

- Antarctic Prion
- Arctic Tern
- Southern Giant Petrel
- Short-tailed Shearwater
- Snowy Sheathbill
- Slender-billed Prion
- Antarctic Tern
- Sooty Shearwater
- Wandering Albatross
- Royal Albatross
- Southern Fulmar
- Flesh-footed Shearwater
- Northern Giant Petrel
- Cape Petrel
- Antarctic Petrel
- White-headed Petrel
- Snow Petrel
- Mottled Petrel
- Soft-plumaged Petrel
- White-chinned Petrel
- Blue Petrel
- Fairy Prion
- Broad-billed Prion
- Kelp Gull
- Antarctic Shag
- Blue-eyed Shag
- Slender-billed Prion
- Common diving Petrel (Drake)
- Wilson's Storm Petrel
- Black bellied Storm-Petrel
- White-faced Storm-Petrel
- Gray-backed Storm-Petrel
- South Polar Skua
- Brown Skua
- Long-tailed Jaeger

Very soon we will be publishing a *Guide of Animal Identification in Antarctica*.

360 Pictures

Scan these QR codes to see Antarctica in 360!

Navigating Lemaire Channel

Zodiac among ice pieces

Leaving Lemaire Channel

Zodiac cruising

Admiring an ice arch

Zodiacs among icebergs

About the Authors

Paula Ford was born in Buenos Aires and is married to Gerardo Bartolomé. She's a Biologist and a member of the Argentine National Scientific and Technical Research Council, with numerous scientific papers to her name.

Gerardo, also from Buenos Aires, is a Civil Engineer. Since 2005, he has authored several books on Argentina's history. In 2018, he founded EDICIONES HISTÓRICAS, an independent publishing company.

Recently, Paula has taken on photography, and Gerardo continues to write. Together, they're publishing travel guides, sharing their country's knowledge with fellow travelers. This led to the creation of "Be There Guides," essential for those exploring the southern part of South America.

89957746R10056